LITTLE PINK PIGS AND OTHER CONVERSATIONS

Allyson Parker

LITTLE PINK PIGS AND OTHER CONVERSATIONS

THE HEART AND CULTURE OF CHILDREN'S MINISTRY

ALLYSON PARKER

Little Pink Pigs and Other Conversations by Allyson Parker
Copyright ©2020 by Allyson Parker
All Rights Reserved.
ISBN: 978-1-59755-609-5

Published by: ADVANTAGE BOOKS™ Longwood, Florida, USA

This book and parts thereof may not be reproduced in any form, stored in a retrieval system or transmitted in any form by any means (electronic, mechanical, photocopy, recording or otherwise) without prior written permission of the author, except as provided by United States of America copyright law.

Scripture quotations marked (CEV) are from the Contemporary English Version Copyright © 1991, 1992, 1995 by American Bible Society. Used by Permission.

Scripture quotations marked ERV are from the Easy-to-Read Version (ERV), International Edition © 2013, 2016 by Bible League International and used by permission.

Scripture quotations marked MSG are from *The Message*. Copyright © 1993, 1994, 1995, 1996, 2000, 2001, 2002. Used by permission of NavPress Publishing Group.

Scripture quotations marked (NIV) are taken from the Holy Bible, New International Version®, NIV®. Copyright © 1973, 1978, 1984, 2011 by Biblica, Inc.™ Used by permission of Zondervan. All rights reserved worldwide. www.zondervan.com The "NIV" and "New International Version" are trademarks registered in the United States Patent and Trademark Office by Biblica, Inc.™

Scripture quotations marked (NIrV) are taken from the Holy Bible, New International Reader's Version®, NIrV® Copyright © 1995, 1996, 1998, 2014 by Biblica, Inc.™ Used by permission of Zondervan. All rights reserved worldwide. www.zondervan.com The "NIrV" and "New International Reader's Version" are trademarks registered in the United States Patent and Trademark Office by Biblica, Inc.™

Scripture quotations marked (NLT) are taken from the Holy Bible, New Living Translation, copyright © 1996, 2004, 2007, 2013, 2015 by Tyndale House Foundation. Used by permission of Tyndale House Publishers, Inc., Carol Stream, Illinois 60188. All rights reserved.

Scripture quotations marked TPT are from The Passion Translation®. Copyright © 2017, 2018 by Passion & Fire Ministries, Inc. Used by permission. All rights reserved. ThePassionTranslation.com.

Library of Congress Catalog Number: 2020951166

First Printing: December 2020
20 21 22 23 24 25   10 9 8 7 6 5 4 3 2 1
Printed in the United States of America

Table of Contents

INTRODUCTION 7

A HAY BALE AND A WHISPERED PRAYER 9

A LITTLE GIRL WITH NO NAME 11

YABBIES AND A FUTURE KING 13

HERE'S ONE I PREPARED EARLIER 17

SNAKES IN THE DUNNY 21

YVES ST LAURENT MEETS 23

COWBOYS AND INDIANS 23

BUT FIRST, COFFEE…. 27

FOR THE FUN OF THE JOY 31

PERMISSION TO SHINE 33

TOE JAM WITH LIFE LESSONS 37

THE BED AND THE BEARDED DRAGON 41

GRASSHOPPERS AND BIRTHDAY CAKE 45

A HORSE, SOME RAIN, SOME BREAD AND HOME 49

LITTLE PINK PIGS 53

SLEEPWALKING DILEMMAS 57

Allyson Parker

Introduction

I'm not sure how you decide that what you have to say should be written into a book. To be honest, this has been an internal argument for me for the past 12 months.

I recognize there are far greater and more skilled leaders than myself; people with an ability to think strategically, develop ministry systems and lead hundreds of volunteers over multi-site campuses with apparent ease. There are those with far greater education in multiple fields and those with incredible creativity and artistry. Without any false humility, why would it matter what I think? How could anything I have experienced add to the myriad of brilliant Children's Ministry resources available at the click of a button?

I still don't know. But the gentle pushing of the Holy Spirit has me writing despite my arguments and insecurity.

So this is not a leadership book nor a children's ministry training manual. It is the conversations we would have if we caught up for coffee and started talking about the greatest calling and passion of my life: ministry to children.

My only prayer is that in whatever way He chooses, Holy Spirit would bring fresh encouragement and vision to you through these conversations and that Jesus would be the absolute centre of all you do.

Allyson Parker

A Hay Bale and a Whispered Prayer

There's a lot about my childhood that I don't remember clearly. There's great pictures and moments- but not months and years of childhood. We moved a lot. I attended 7 schools between Kindergarten and Year 12. I don't have recollections of long term familiar places or family and friends living close by. However, I vividly remember sitting on top of a big hay bale at eleven years of age, in the middle of a paddock on a farm way out of Goondiwindi in Queensland and whispering to a God I knew of, but barely knew, "I want my life to count for something."

It was a seemingly impossible prayer. It was rare for me to go to church for a number of reasons, not least of which was, "Was there a church to go to?" Yet here I was, an incredibly shy and insecure little country kid, from a poor family, sitting in the middle of no-where, wanting to change the world with no earthly possibility of actually making that happen. There was nothing about me or my life that would make anyone consider that the Saviour of the world would choose me for anything, yet as we know:

1 Corinthians 1:27 The Passion Translation (TPT)

²⁷ But God chose those whom the world considers foolish to shame those who think they are wise, and God chose the puny and powerless to shame the high and mighty.

God puts eternity in our hearts. We're designed to live life with the purpose and passion of heaven no matter who we are.

My Mum loved Jesus with all her heart and she never gave up on praying for me. At 23 I was born again and that whispered prayer from so long past found life again. At 24 years of age, the Holy Spirit called me into children's ministry with one simple sentence, "Bring me the children." It was a sentence that was to transform every part of my life and its focus. It was to define my purpose, and, to this day, God has not re-directed my life away from this.

The profound difference between the child on the hay bale and the sense of significance, purpose and privilege I feel in my life from what God is allowing me to do now, becomes sharper with each passing year. I remain very aware of my own 'ordinariness' that coexists alongside the truth of who I am in Christ. It is, at times, an uncomfortable mental coexistence.

You, like me, are probably well aware of your flaws and shortcomings. You know your background, mistakes and weaknesses. Not one of us will ever see ourselves exactly as God does when we look at ourselves through the lens of the past or the opinion of our self or others. You may have heard it many times before, but let me remind you again, 'God is not looking for the perfect. He's looking for those who would dare to whisper, "I want my life to count for something", then choose to pursue what He calls them to, however falteringly, with all their heart.

This is true of the children you minister to. There are those whose family situation and ministry 'pedigree' would seem to position them for greatness in the Kingdom, and those who rarely attend and may outwardly, for whatever reason, present as 'unlikely to change the world'. Yet God will hear all their prayers from the bold and audacious to the timid, impossible, unrealistic whispered cries of small hearts. Only time will truly tell the story of what the King of Heaven does in answer to them all. For now, you get to hold those hearts and help inspire the dreams and prayers that may come from them. Help them see beyond themselves and dream of bringing the Kingdom here on earth. May they each whisper, "I want my life to count for something' and may that 'something' have an eternal focus.

Reflect

- What is the Kingdom vision you give your children?
- How well do you help them focus beyond themselves?

A Little Girl With No Name

A little girl entered my world and left it again just 1 hour later. I don't remember her name. I was working in emergency and she came in via ambulance.

Her family were refugees from Vietnam. They hadn't been in Australia long. Their English was limited and they did not know how to call an ambulance. Their 10 year old daughter was having an asthma attack. By the time they got a neighbour to help, she was no longer breathing.

For an hour we tried to resuscitate her. We tried everything. But nothing we did brought any kind of life. This little girl died.

Resuscitating anyone is difficult. It is confronting. There's raw emotion and desperation mixed with professional skill and pragmatism. There's calm efficiency whilst making absolute life and death decisions that will profoundly impact a family. There's medical noise and mess followed by outpoured grief. Both the fragility and preciousness of life comes rushing to the forefront of your consciousness.

Children are a whole new level of difficult. They are not meant to die- that is meant to be the realm of the old and frail. For me, her death came with a stark and overwhelming reality of eternity.

Her family were Buddhist. She had never heard the name of Jesus. She never knew the hope of heaven. She had never heard that healing was in his Name. She never saw the feet of those who bring Good News.

Not once.

There may be many great theologians who could argue their position on whether or not she went to heaven. To me, this is *almost* irrelevant.

She deserved to know about Jesus. She deserved the chance to hear. She should have had the choice to follow him, to hear his voice and encounter his love. She should have been able to turn to him in the time of her greatest need. She should have had the hope of heaven.

It's that simple.

1 John 5:12 New International Version (NIV)

^{12} Whoever has the Son has life; whoever does not have the Son of God does not have life.

We now have a generation of children in Australia who are as lost as this little girl. They have never heard the Name of Jesus. They know nothing of God or the Bible. George Barna has done some incredible research that clearly points to the profound value of ministry to children- not just in the now, but for the long-term health of the church. Take time to read it. It will inspire you and encourage you in your ministry calling.

However, as inspiring as the research is, I found in my life that stats and research could also fill my heart with pride (children's ministry is the most important ministry) and resentment (if others knew how important children's ministry was then……).

But doing CPR on a tiny human body stripped this all away. The only thing that mattered was, "Did she know about Jesus?"

Not all the children in your community will make it to old age. They may die before youth group. Across the nations of the world, children are not only one of the biggest 'people groups', but also one of the most vulnerable to death through disease, exploitation or conflict. If God has called you to reach them, don't wait for the world to cheer you on to do it.

God has entrusted you.

And they deserve to know.

It's that simple.

Reflect

- What holds me back from reaching children with the gospel?
- Are these real barriers, or limitations I have assumed?

Yabbies and a Future King

In 1981 I gave the future King of England a yabbie caught in the dam near my house.

Well, actually the security team gave him the yabbie dutifully brought to him by my Dad and gifted to him not only by myself, but from all my sisters as well.

We lived on a farm 60kms out of Moree in NSW, and the property owner, Sinclair Hill, just happened to be Prince Charles' polo coach. The Prince of Wales was visiting Australia after his recent engagement to Lady Diana, and had come to stay on the farm during a weekend break from royal duties. Sinclair arranged for a barbeque with the staff, their families and the Prince. As you can imagine, there was considerable excitement and some attending the barbeque desperately wanted to have the attention of the Prince. My sisters and I did not fall into this category. We were bored, so we took a couple of lamb chops off the table, found some bale-o-twine in the back of the ute and headed off to the dam that was nearby to catch yabbies. The Prince noticed, left the barbeque and came with us. For probably 30 minutes we all tried to entice a yabbie from the water, but failed, and His Royal Highness seemed to express genuine disappointment because of this. The Prince was required back with the other guests and we went home, determined to rectify our failure for the sake of the Prince. It was with great delight that we secured a yabbie on the line in the dam near our house, and we insisted that Prince Charles really wanted it and it should be delivered to His Royal Highness along with the milk the next morning. Dad graciously agreed and delivered our gift to the security team. Apparently Prince Charles was 'chuffed'.

I laugh when I think about this now. As if the future King of England ever wanted or needed a yabbie given to him by four little bush kids! Our childish perception of this was ridiculous. Nevertheless, he was kind enough to make us feel as though he did and we genuinely believed this because he went out of his way to take time for us and make us feel important.

I often think about this as I look at what I offer the King of Heaven. As if anything you or I can bring Him can really add anything to Him in any way- and yet he so kindly allows us to feel as though it does. We are given the privilege of serving in His Kingdom. He graciously endows us with gifts and talents to use for Him. He anoints and empowers us for ministry and plans good works for us to do in advance. Honestly, all we do, all we give, all we are proud of, are 'yabbies for a King', but if we have the same passionate delight in bringing them to our Saviour as my sisters and I did in presenting a yabbie to Prince Charles, He sees our heart and receives our offering with great love. Through this grace, we genuinely can play a significant role in seeing His Kingdom advancing in the world. There is great wonder in this, as the Psalmist writes:

Psalm 8:4-6 The Passion Translation (TPT)

> *[4] Compared to all this cosmic glory, why would you bother with puny, mortal man or be infatuated with Adam's sons? [5] Yet what honour you have given to men, created only a little lower than Elohim, crowned like kings and queens with glory and magnificence.*
>
> *[6] You have delegated to them mastery over all you have made, making everything subservient to their authority, placing earth itself under the feet of your image-bearers.*

There are times though, that pride in what we achieve or accomplish in ministry begins to rear its ugly head. [How easily my sinful nature wanders down this familiar path!] We may start out in humility, but somewhere, along the way, with a bit of success, we begin to compare our ministry to another; our numbers of attendees to someone else's; our team recruitment or training with those around us even though Isaiah reminds us:

Isaiah 64:6a Contemporary English Version (CEV)

⁶ We are unfit to worship you; each of our good deeds is merely a filthy rag.

When we find ourselves in the place of comparison or competition, then we need to remember "yabbies for a king" and allow true thankfulness that He would choose us, to fill our heart once more, and real humility direct our steps again.

Prince Charles noticed my sisters and me and took time for us- something we neither expected, nor deserved in any way. We received his undivided attention and what we believed about ourselves, and therefore, the significance of our lives in relation to his, changed because of it.

Each of us, as children's ministers, have the chance to leave the 'barbeque of ministry tasks, parent demands and team friendships' to notice and take time for children who are disengaged, disconnected and feel insignificant or unimportant. A conversation, undivided attention, a word of encouragement, truly joining in with a child's game, focus or interest, getting down to a child's eye level or the genuine acceptance of a childish gift (my favourite so far has been a bunch of sticks tied with a ribbon and presented as flowers) can transform a child's perspective and life.

We are Christ's ambassadors- and for a child that means that how we interact with them, cannot be separated from their God concept and how they see themselves in relation to Him. How you speak- he speaks. What you do- Jesus does.

"Quality time" is not just a parenting catch phrase, it is the manifestation of the heart of Jesus for children. It matters and it will have a permanent significance in the life of a child well beyond their childhood.

Reflect

- Do I humbly honour the privilege of ministry I have been given?
- Do I take time for children in the midst of the tasks of ministry in a way that makes them feel significant?

Allyson Parker

Here's One I Prepared Earlier

I am an Australian MasterChef fan. I love the creativity. I love the positivity. I love the apparent support both judges and contestants give each other. [Please don't burst my idealistic bubble- I like my final edit viewing]. I love the moment in a pressure test when the dish the contestants have to cook is revealed. It's the ultimate 'here's one I prepared earlier' disclosure. There's a moment of awe as the contestants take time to look at the finished product. From there, they get to taste, and then the contestants are given the recipe, required cooking utensils and ingredients in order to recreate that dish as closely as they possibly can.

Jesus is God's ultimate 'here's one I prepared earlier' example. We look at his life, his words and his actions with wondrous awe as we understand we are meant to become like him in our own lives. The Bible literally teaches us to taste and see that He is good! We sample His goodness and savour His presence. We experience the exquisitely complex 'flavours' of his multifaceted love, mercy, grace, kindness, sternness and strength. And then he gives us the required recipe (Word), utensils (Holy Spirit) and ingredients (forgiveness, redemption, adoption, love and the family of God) in order for us to reproduce who He is in our own lives. For us (thankfully) it's never a pressure test.

I have to admit that when I started in my Children's Pastor role, I was 'cooking' more like a contestant with a 'mystery box' challenge. There were a few ingredients I could choose from, but ultimately the outcome was my creation. I inherited a ministry that was challenging. I wasn't sure if team would show up and the greatest goal of the 10-12 year olds was to leave. So my first plan was 'to make it fun'. Now don't misunderstand me. I'm all for fun (we'll have a conversation about this), but there was no clear intentionality in the program in regards to the long term discipleship outcomes I wanted to lay the foundation for. Our program was much more like a random 'mystery box' week to week and month to month. Until I read about a children's ministry in the USA that literally closed its program for six months as they considered the following:

If a child had been part of their children and youth ministries yet still wasn't able to take their place in the army of God, what had they produced? Could they honestly say their ministry was successful? They asked themselves, "If, after 7-18 years of ministry, their children…

- Could not hear the voice of God
- Didn't know what it was to be led by the Spirit
- Didn't know how to pray for the sick
- Didn't know how to walk in faith
- Didn't have a relevant devotional life
- Couldn't share their faith
- Couldn't take their place as prayer warriors and worshippers

…then what were they capable of doing in the kingdom of God?"

What good was it if each child knew how many stones David picked up to kill Goliath if they did not have a real relationship with Jesus?

It was a moment that the Holy Spirit literally had me standing still. What was I doing? What was I aiming for? How was I stewarding what I had been entrusted with- the very foundational discipleship of the next generation?

I would add to this list:

- What if our kids don't know what the Great Commission is, and why this is their life purpose even if manifest through differing talents and ministry expressions?
- What if they don't have a heart to be generous?

Children are in our hands. This is their most teachable time in life. This is when they are forming the very foundations of faith, morality, ethics and worldview. This is when they will choose if life is about them, or if life is about others and the purpose for which God created them. This is when they are deciding the significance of Jesus' death and resurrection in their own lives. What sort of disciples will leave our ministry?

God has given us everything we need in order to reproduce Jesus in our own lives- and He has entrusted us with the genesis of this in the lives of the next generation using the same tools of faith. Don't flit from one program or idea to the next. Sit down, think about and plan the deliberate faith foundations you will aim to establish in kids' lives and program from there.

Plan the fun….. but first plan Jesus.

Reflect:

- Do I have a clear discipleship plan and goal for children who are involved in my ministry?
- Have I thoughtfully arranged my program and communicated with my team in order to achieve this?
- What are the strategies I have in place to assist parents to disciple their children at home?

Allyson Parker

Little Pink Pigs and Other Conversations

Snakes in the Dunny

When we lived on a farm out of the tiny town of Trangie in NSW, we had an outside toilet. The toilet was one that flushed, but was located probably 4 metres off the back of the house. In the winter it was freezing, but in the long, hot summer it was a cool, slightly damp place of respite from the Australian sun and a particularly favourite place of rest for both brown and red-belly black snakes.

Large ones.

Highly venomous, 'we will most certainly kill you' ones.

So there were some very important toilet rules in our household-

- Rule #1: Don't hang on too long if you need to use the loo. If there's a snake (highly likely), it will be a paddock run for you.
- Rule #2: Push the door gently. If you hear a rustling sound behind the door DO NOT ENTER.
- Rule #3: Pray Dad kills the snake before it gets a chance to move [this was before the days of protection of snakes. We never noticed any kind of snake shortage…..]
- Rule #4: Place dispatched snake on the meat ants' nest for a few days. You'll be sure to get a great skeleton for 'show and tell' at school (which will be a hit with the boys, but may make your teacher slightly faint).

The enemy will always try to make himself comfortable in the vulnerable, but comfortable places in our 'life house'; those places in our lives that we have not yet brought into submission and obedience to Christ. He'll settle in until we are prepared to open the door to that area and allow the Father to come and dispatch him. Too often in my life I've chosen the easier 'paddock run' option, rather than opening the door to the places the enemy still holds strong. I've not wanted to run the risk of facing the enemy.

The craziest thing about this is, that just as my Dad dealt with the snakes in the dunny at home, it's my Dad in Heaven who will deal with the 'snakes' in my soul even now. And just as we used to get great skeletons for show and tell in the classroom, as we allow the Holy Spirit to deal with our bondages, brokenness, fears and failures, we'll have some fabulous 'skeletons' of the enemy to display in our testimony. [I'm not talking bringing out the skeletons in our closet in an awkward 'too much information' way- but rather clearly testifying of the evidence of the defeat of the enemy through the power of the blood of Jesus and the transformation the Holy Spirit has brought to our heart and life.]

So here's some simple life rules-

- Rule #1: Don't hang on too long with the enemy comfortable in your space.
- Rule #2: If a gentle push (or a big one) reveals the 'rustle of the enemy' in your response, go get Dad.
- Rule #3: Pray.
- Rule #4: Show and tell the work of God in your life.
- Rule #5: Teach this to your kids.

Reflect:

- How can I implement these rules?
- How can I teach them to the next generation?

Yves St Laurent Meets Cowboys and Indians

My Aunty Pauline was not a biological Aunt. She was my Mum's best friend from childhood. She would never have auditioned for 'Farmer wants a Wife'. For her, farm life was something to quickly visit and rapidly retreat from- back to the cleanliness and comforts of the city. She had perfect hair, perfect makeup and perfect nails. These were not attributes that were necessarily highly prized when getting the cow in I have to admit, but Aunty Pauline was determined that my sisters and I should experience some of the feminine delights of having makeup. She came to visit us when we were living out of Barraba in NSW, bringing with her a range of her old makeup including a variety of shades of expensive lipsticks. We were so excited. She explained the contents and gave us a demonstration of their use. We took the gift with great thankfulness and headed off. Aunty Pauline sat with my Mum to have a cup of tea, and eat something delicious my Mum had baked, to await the 'great makeover reveal.'

The time passed. We did not return perhaps as quickly as expected. Then, in the background, there came the sounds of Native American war cries (well at least our Australian, undoubtedly completely culturally inappropriate rendition of said war cries due to 1970's movies) from the back yard. Mum and Aunty Pauline came out, and to Aunty Pauline's absolute horror, we had used the expensive lipsticks to paint some fearsome war paints on each other prior to engaging in an epic game of 'Cowboys and Indians'. I think she left in despair of us ever becoming 'ladies.'

So often we are limited by our expectations, traditions, time constraints, experience and adult perspective and responsibilities. We allow the mundane and routine to steal joy, passion and fun out of both the secular and the sacred. We don't see the possibilities or engage in creativity because we always do what we always do- simply because we don't look for anything else. Lipstick is for lips, right?

But what if lipstick could be for war paint, art, sculpture, hopscotch, mini bowling pins or fake blood?

God is the most creative, out- of- the box thinker there is and the Bible says:

1 Corinthians 2:16 New International Reader's Version (NIRV)

[16] "Who can ever know what is in the Lord's mind? Can anyone ever teach him?" But we have the mind of Christ.

I have the mind of Christ! (This is something I frequently remind my Pastor of.)

You also have the mind of Christ and one of the simplest ways to activate the creativity within is to incorporate multiple intelligence learning styles throughout your ministry program.

I believe we must incorporate digital technology with our tech savvy generation.

But I also believe we should incorporate taste, touch, smell, and other sight and sound.

There should be room for Bible stories as musicals or rhyming poems.

Or 'books with no pictures' (If you have not read The Book with no Pictures by BJ Novak there is something missing in your life!)

Or re-written (with Biblical accuracy) as 'Hairy Tales' (because there are no fairy tales in the Bible, but once upon a time, a long, long time ago…) and dramatically presented so as to have kids laughing with life-long memories.

There should be room for interpersonal and intrapersonal reflection plus analytical data analysis- otherwise known as the facts and timelines.

There should be a place for questions and questioning as well as art, music, dance, rhythm and science.

Kids should get dirty and messy (how will they ever survive a Missions trip to the third world if they freak out at the smallest amount of mess or potential 'germs'?)

They should be able to take calculated risks.

Their ideas should have a voice. Have afternoon tea with your kids and ask for their opinion and ideas.

Take time to let your own imagination run wild.
What could be possible if a lipstick was not for lips?

Reflect:

- Where has ministry become mundane, routine and repetitive?
- What new creative element could bring fresh life to how you minister?

Allyson Parker

But First, Coffee....

I have an addiction- and a great love. "But first coffee" is not a cute sign in my office, it's a reality of my life.

I have to confess I have become a coffee snob. There's only certain beans I like, coffee chains I avoid and I even have a preference for the brand, frothiness and amount of milk. I don't drink cappuccinos- don't put chocolate powder on the top of my coffee. Ewww. I'm convinced that there is a conspiracy with all airport managements to only allow the very worst coffee within the terminal to ensure that people catch their flight, not sit around enjoying the cafes. My life is now a far cry from the desperate days of night shift in emergency when even the cheapest instant coffee (what even is that stuff?) would suffice in order to drive home safely.

As I said, I inherited a challenging ministry when I took on the Children's Pastor's position at my church. I was well aware that I did not have the skill set to bring any significant change and so I had a choice in that season of 'ministry desperation'. I could settle for the 'instant' or seek the 'real'. I could work out of my own strength (which was minimal) or go deeper. I chose the latter. I fasted for 40 hours a week for 40 weeks and I set a 10 year vision before God. I wish I could tell you that there was immediate dramatic change, exponential growth and miraculous team building. There wasn't. But that's the nature of a foundation, isn't it? It is unseen, often for months before the final structure begins to take shape. I know that what I see now was built upon that initial foundation as I pursued the Holy Spirit.

For me personally, it was to shift me from ever really being satisfied with the 'instant' versions of ministry and relationship with Jesus. I have become, unashamedly, a 'Holy Spirit snob'. I need Him. I want Him. I yearn to see the outpouring of His Presence in our services. I want children to walk in the love, knowledge, power, authority and purpose of Christ, and this is something I cannot develop in them through my skill set- this is entirely the work of the Holy Spirit.

I wish I could confess that my need for the power, presence and leading of the Holy Spirit was always, equally, a requirement in my life. How is it that we somehow drift into thinking we can do life, relationships, parenting, work or ministry without a desperate need of Him first? Why do we settle for the 'cheap instant coffee' or 'airport terminal' spiritual experience, when there is the possibility of something far more real and satisfying? I know in my life this happens when I allow 'world creep' into my soul. I take my eyes off heaven and Jesus' face and find myself distracted by the world around me. It is, essentially idolatry. But Jesus, in his grace, is merciful, every time we return to our first love.

You only need a genuine, humble desire to minister to the needs of others to begin to move in the power and anointing of the Holy Spirit. Spiritual disciplines that release the gifts of the Holy Spirit in our lives are a free choice for every follower of Jesus to pursue, no matter their title (or lack thereof), position, ministry, age, education or experience. Every time I choose to seek the Father and require him as my first love, the foundation upon which all my life and ministry is built, strengthens and deepens. The stronger the foundation, the more that can be built upon it.

The Apostle Paul said:

1 Corinthians 2:4 Contemporary English Version (CEV)

⁴ When I talked with you or preached, I didn't try to prove anything by sounding wise. I simply let God's Spirit show his power.

Our children can find far greater 'entertainment' than we can provide them outside of the church. But they are unlikely to ever experience the life –changing power of the Holy Spirit outside of the body of Christ. Let their first experience of the Holy Spirit be while they are still young. Nothing weird or fearsome- but the beautiful, powerful, life transforming, bondage- breaking, oil of the Holy Spirit flowing from the anointing upon your life that causes them to know without doubt that God is real and miracles are possible. Create space for Him to move and learn to lean in to the smallest whisper to step out in faith. Desire the gifts of the Spirit. This is not ungodly or vain if motivated by love. This is your God-given privilege. Be courageous enough to step beyond, "I'm JUST a children's leader", to "I am a minister of God." Learn to recognize the manifestation of the Spirit in your life and steward this anointing well.

Saturate your ministry and your children in prayer. It is arrogant of us to expect the Holy Spirit to come at our demand, if we will not humble ourselves and first enthrone him and prepare the 'sanctuary' for His Presence. In the Old Testament, the priests carried the weight of the Ark upon their shoulders. They positioned it in its rightful place within the temple. It was a physical honour to have that duty that only a select few were born into. Ours is a birthright we all gain through Christ. We must carry it with equal honour. In the past 12 months my key leaders and I have started to pray from 6:30-7:20am before any of the other team arrive each Sunday. Then we pray as a team. Have we seen a dramatic change, exponential growth in kids' numbers or miraculous team building? Not yet. But what it is doing in us is far more significant at this stage. What is built from this foundation in our children and team is yet to be manifest, but it is coming. There's a new 10 year plan- and, because of those first 40 weeks when I first started, an incredible team to carry it forward far, far beyond anything I could do. I dare you to make this your prayer:

Psalm 63:1-2 The Passion Translation (TPT)

¹ O God of my life, I'm lovesick for you in this weary wilderness. I thirst with the deepest longings to love you more, with cravings in my heart that can't be described. Such yearning grips my soul for you, my God! ² I'm energized every time I enter your heavenly sanctuary to seek more of your power and drink in more of your glory.

Reflect:

- Is my ministry built on gifts, talent and hard work alone- or founded on seeking God?

- Do I expect God to show up, or do I choose to create a throne room for him to move within?

- Do I see myself as a minister- or JUST a children's leader?

Allyson Parker

Little Pink Pigs and Other Conversations

For the Fun of the Joy

It was Sunday morning and one or our pre-schoolers was doing something- I can't even remember exactly what it was. Whatever she was doing elicited the question, "Why are you doing that?" The child looked up, smiled, and responded, "For the fun of the joy."

It has become a catch phrase of our ministry ever since.

"For the fun of the joy"- or just because it's fun, is one of the great privileges of Children's Ministry. As passionate as I am about ensuring there is clear discipleship purpose in teaching content, as well as a powerful Presence of the Holy Spirit, I am equally passionate that there is a whole heap of fun.

If the kids' ministry is the Department of Boring, we might as well all pack up and go home. Kids won't want to come, team won't want to be there and the long term prospect of the church is in jeopardy. (Yes, that dramatic- remember we get to captivate little hearts for Jesus; help them develop their God concept and learn to love His church.)

I honestly believe that serving Jesus through His church should be the best time in anyone's week, so this should make being on the Kids' team truly one of the best teams to be involved in. I regularly tell people I have the best job in the world. I get to tell a generation about Jesus. I may see their first decision for Christ or experience a moment of wonder in worship as they encounter the Holy Spirit personally, and I also get to play games and eat lollies.

So play games as part of the intentionality of engagement in teaching content- but also just do stuff 'for the fun of the joy'- because this is what kids do. And this is what kids love.

- Throw tinned tomatoes in a fan- at least once in your life.
- Play cheerio face off- slather your friend's face in margarine and roll it in cheerios [pro tip: avoid eyes, nostrils and ears with the margarine].

- Build giant plastic bucket walls and crash through them like superman.
- Do a colour run.
- Build box forts.
- Have sword fights with bread sticks.
- Stick a square of chocolate on the end of your tongue and see how long it takes to melt.
- Try to gargle a song and have your team guess what the song is. [no laughing allowed]
- Roll down a hill or slide down on cardboard sheets.
- Make lamingtons with your feet.

"Steal" ideas, adapt other games, set a theme and see what creativity ensues, ask for help, BUT MOST IMPORTANTLY, join in, play too, FOR THE FUN OF THE JOY!

Reflect:

- How much fun is our Kids' ministry?
- Where can I go to get ideas or help to add fun?
- Am I willing to do something 'for the fun of the joy' with the children in our kids' ministry?

Little Pink Pigs and Other Conversations

Permission to Shine

I was sitting in a women's ministry Bible Study probably about 1997. The church I attended had amalgamated with another church in a miraculous move of God the year prior. At this point in my life I had little kids, an unsaved husband, and would come in to church, serve in kids and go home so I did not 'get in trouble' from said unsaved husband. (He was radically saved and now serves in kids' ministry. He's still my husband.) I was not well known in the congregation. I must have answered a question somewhat intelligently because the woman leading the study group looked at me and asked, "Where do you serve?" I answered, "In children's ministry" to which she responded, "Oh don't worry, dear. We all have to start somewhere, don't we?"

I can laugh about this now, but at the time, it was another nail in my insecurity coffin. I loved Jesus with all my heart and I passionately wanted to serve him, but I battled with who I was in Him and how others saw me. Talk about snakes in the dunny! I would say that one of the greatest regrets of my life is how long it took me to really begin to allow God to bring healing to this area of my life, and it remains, that who I am in Christ and the flaws and failings I see in me, can still, at times, be an uncomfortable mental co-existence as I have said. I had to battle words that had been spoken over me and that I had appropriated to my life. I had to renew my mind about what I believed about me- but mostly, I had to learn to let Jesus just love me without trying to be or do anything for Him.

My beautiful friend, Vikki, once said, "Some days I just say to Jesus, 'I'm your favourite, aren't I?'. This statement rocked my world. To know His love like that and to be so confident in it! No self- flagellation, self-deprecation, or internal condemnation. She walked in a freedom of truth I had never known despite years of following Jesus. Of course it is a statement that is both entirely true and completely false all at once. If God sees Jesus in me- then I'm his favourite. At the same time, God has no favourites- all are equal in his sight. But the revelation opened a whole new world for me; a world in which I learnt to give **myself** permission to shine.

Matthew 5:14-16 New Living Translation (NLT)

[14] "You are the light of the world—like a city on a hilltop that cannot be hidden. [15] No one lights a lamp and then puts it under a basket. Instead, a lamp is placed on a stand, where it gives light to everyone in the house. [16] In the same way, let your good deeds shine out for all to see, so that everyone will praise your heavenly Father.

Our lives are meant to light the world.
Our lives are meant to light our **House.**
Our lives are meant to light other's lives.
Our lives are meant to throw a spotlight onto our Heavenly Father.
Our lives are meant to stand out.

And yet, even hearing this now, may make you feel emotional or uncomfortable. You may be hiding under some of the 'baskets' that cover all God is calling you to be, that I also had to throw off:

The basket of identity

Do you ask yourself, "Who am I'? Do you repeat the lie, 'God would never choose me'? Do you say, even in your head, 'I'm not good enough'? Have the words, 'You're nothing' been spoken over you and settled in your heart? Do you see yourself through the lens of salvation and position in Christ, or through the lens of rejection? Is your self image based in the Word or what family, friends or workmates see?

According to public perception, Jesus was just the son of the carpenter Joseph. Imagine if Jesus had lived limited by what his family/ friends saw. What if Jesus had chosen to not believe what was written about him and what he was told about God and his destiny? What if he let his natural identity define and limit him rather than live out the truth of who He really was?

It's a choice we have as well. Just like Jesus, we can choose to live out of our 'natural' identity- or out of the truth written in the Word, the purpose for which God designed us and what He says about us. In doing so, we will either live limited or fulfil the plan God has for our lives.

The basket of insecurity

Different to who you see yourself as, this one is about what you think you can do- but so often, identity and insecurity link arms and don't let go.

The basket of opinions

Woven into this basket is fear of failure, intimidation, striving, need for recognition, pride, the hurt of criticism, comparison and any number of other nasties all jostling for mind position and restraining rights- so throwing this one off has the ability to let some serious freedom enter your world.

This week I was asked by a NSW Government Department for my feedback and advice on a document they were preparing for the governance boards of organisations under their jurisdiction. That's a galactic leap from a hay bale in the paddock of nowhere! Nothing in my life stems from my education, any remarkable giftedness or societal position. All that I am, I owe to my Saviour and all he has done in my life. But I had to give myself permission to shine for Him- not stay in the shadows of my past.

There will be people who will despise how, when, where, and what we do to serve God. They will question our motives, our time, our capacity, our ability and mostly the 'importance' of what we do. And there will be those who will honour us. But in the end, to really shine, settle in your heart that all you do is for an audience of One. In the end He's the one with the eternal crowns!

Take your place on the stand God has positioned you and light it up.

And in doing so, give permission for your kids to do the same.

Reflect:
- Have I given myself permission to be all God has called me to be?
- Do I let Jesus love me?

Toe Jam with Life Lessons

I failed showering the first time I was assessed on this skill when I trained as a nurse.

How is that even possible you may wonder? It's not exactly rocket science.

I thought so too, but in failing I learnt a life lesson that has become a core principle of who I am.

My first practical nursing placement was in an aged care home. The college I attended deliberately did this so that they would identify those whose heart was to serve- and those whose motivation was not what they were looking for. My nursing supervisor was old school- and exceptional. Beds had to be made with precision, speed and perfectly creased hospital corners. She had no time for laziness, carelessness or "I can't do it." I'm so grateful to her- for what she taught me professionally- and for what she taught me for life.

She supervised me showering an elderly lady. We were assessed on infection control as well as the care and the dignity with which we treated people. I got to the end of the shower and she asked if I was finished. I had washed my patient completely. I had followed all infection control procedures. I had spoken to her with care and consideration throughout. To be honest, I thought I had done a great job really. So I said, "yes". She looked at me and then said, "Ok. Well then you fail this assessment. Let me show you why."

She spoke gently and with such respect to the elderly woman and asked if she could show me what I'd missed. At the woman's consent, she got down and asked me to look between her toes. I'm glad you can't smell what I smelt- or envisage what I saw. Between her toes was a disgusting build up of brown gunge, which when gently cleaned away, revealed raw, infected skin. No one had properly cleaned her feet for months at least. Our patient cried- both from pain and from thankfulness.

My clinical supervisor turned to me and said, "She deserves better than this. She deserves someone to treat her as though she is their own grandmother and wash her with the care that prevents this happening. She can't move her toes apart any more. She needs you to do what she cannot do."

She deserves better than this. She needs you to do what she cannot do."

I've never forgotten this- not while nursing, nor as a life lesson.

John 13:12-17 MSG

12-17 Then he said, "Do you understand what I have done to you? You address me as 'Teacher' and 'Master,' and rightly so. That is what I am. So if I, the Master and Teacher, washed your feet, you must now wash each other's feet. ***I've laid down a pattern for you. What I've done, you do.*** *I'm only pointing out the obvious. A servant is not ranked above his master; an employee doesn't give orders to the employer. If you understand what I'm telling you, act like it—and live a blessed life.*

Somehow, I think we often think that 'washing each other's feet' is some sort of somewhat romantic spiritual activity. If I speak to you encouragingly, or quickly pray for you, somehow I've washed your feet. Or, even better, if I've attended a deeply spiritual retreat and actually swooshed a bit of water over your (not very dirty, toe jam free) feet and dried them, then I've really washed your feet.

But is this the example Christ gave us?

Not really.

He took off his outer garment and got down to wash the filthy, smelly, feet of men who were to betray him, abandon him, doubt him and let him down. He got down to do what no one else was prepared to do. He became undignified, taking the position of the lowest servant to give us an example to follow- a picture as indelible as my experience of failing foot washing. He chose servanthood.

Ministry is about serving. Nothing more. Nothing less. At its best, it is the powerful combination of a heart motivated by love and a commitment to excellence. True servanthood is quite prepared to become undignified. It never seeks position above people.

Our role is to choose to wash feet through servanthood so parents can thrive, churches can grow and children can be saved.

We do it for those who deserve it and for those who don't.

We do it for each other in our teams.

There is no separating true servanthood from hard work and there is no separating true servanthood from second mile excellence. To think that anything I do that is 'just enough', or completed for attention, recognition or just because someone is watching, is the servanthood that Jesus calls me to, is to delude myself. I think one of the scriptures I have the greatest love/hate relationship with, is:

Colossians 3:23 The Passion Translation (TPT)

²³ Put your heart and soul into every activity you do, as though you are doing it for the Lord himself and not merely for others.

Every time I'm tempted to do 'just enough' I remember that shower assessment and these words come to my heart. I know that there are those who would accuse me of perfectionism- and at times they are right. But mostly, I'm motivated by a life principle that Jesus and others simply deserve my best.

Servanthood in your ministry looks a lot like arriving on time, sweeping the floor and packing equipment away where it came from. Neatly. Every time.

- It manifests as kindness, encouragement, courtesy and consideration.
- It shows itself in humility, forgiveness, grace, patience and mercy.
- It does what is convenient and what is inconvenient. It treats people as precious no matter who they are or what they are capable of doing or giving. It never avoids hard work and does not bring second best. It is very prepared to leave the dignities of adulthood to embrace the undignified actions, music and games

that will introduce kids to Jesus and help them fall in love with Him and His church. It is not motivated by the need for recognition and nor does it push for position.

If there is a bit of a 'fragrance of positioning or "near enough is good enough"' in your life or your team, maybe it's time to remove the 'toe jam' built up due to a lack of servanthood. It may sting for a bit, but the cleansing will save an infection that affects the whole body.

In washing the feet of our children, we may well uncover some 'toe jam' of life- abuse, mental health issues, domestic violence, hurt, fear, anxiety or identity issues. This doesn't happen in the superficial. It happens as we take time, build relationships and trust and deeply care about their lives. Uncovering the brokenness of their lives is hard. But healing can come because of it. May they find in you the hero who will believe them, stand up for them and advocate for their safety. May you do what they cannot do for themselves.

Reflect:

- Does my life reflect foot washing servanthood, or are my motivations for ministry based in need for recognition?
- Does my ministry have the policies and procedures in place to help children if needed?

The Bed and the Bearded Dragon

Father's Day was looming and my sisters and I had no money to spend at the school Father's Day stall. This then created the conundrum of what we could do to solve this dilemma in order to give Dad a Father's Day gift he deserved and would treasure. Being an ingenious bunch, we had noted that there was a large beared dragon that regularly sunned itself on the fencepost on the paddock gate nearby and we decided that undoubtedly Dad would love a bearded dragon as a pet.

We found an old shoe box, just barely big enough to contain our bearded dragon friend and duly, with some effort, caught it on the Saturday prior to Father's Day the next day. We wrapped it up and hid it until the next morning.

Mum and Dad were always up early, so at the crack of dawn all four of us bounded into their bedroom, ensconced ourselves in and on the bed and presented Dad with his gift. I'm not sure who was more surprised at the opening of the box- Dad or the lizard- but both moved fairly rapidly.

Our bearded dragon friend raced off the bed and then under it as we all moved in hot pursuit. We were well practiced in heading off that sheep that tried to move off from the flock, but the dragon was pretty motivated by the need to escape the confines of our house and the box. Somehow, the back door opened (thanks Mum) and our Father's Day gift was last seen running at lightning speed out the back gate. Dad did not seem all that devastated…..

Frequently there is a lament amongst children's ministries regarding the lack of budget to do what we dream of doing.

A lack of budget has created two opportunities in my life:

1. The opportunity to compare, complain, criticise leadership and grow resentment in my soul
2. The opportunity to invest what is in my hand and come up with ingenious solutions

You can probably guess where I'm going with this.

Matthew 6:21 Contemporary English Version (CEV)

²¹ Your heart will always be where your treasure is.

There may be times where our investment into our ministry goes beyond our time and talent. It's not wasted. God sees. Generosity of heart and life is a beautiful characteristic. I'm not suggesting that you don't ask for the budget you need. I'm saying there's always room for an offering that blesses those God has entrusted into your hand if it is needed and you have the capacity to provide it.

If something is beyond both your capacity and the budget, you have just entered the exciting place of both ingenious solutions and the miraculous provision of God. So don't quit dreaming- start praying. Who knows what your testimony will be? There was a time that I was leading a few of our kids' team to Indonesia for a Missions trip. We had been doing all we could to raise the funds we needed to get all the team there. The church policy around handling money always required two people to count any funds. My friend Christine and I were in the office literally counting $5 notes for the trip and at first count we were short. We had no more options- and no more time to raise funds- and a plan to reach hundreds of kids with the gospel. I counted again and there was more than the previous total. She then counted, and once again there was more than the previous total. As the total kept changing, we had to keep counting until each of us had the same result. The final count was exactly what we needed. There were simply, miraculously, more $5 notes with each count, until we had all we needed.

What's in your hand that God could multiply? What ingenious solution could you come up with? What miracle might God provide? Don't lament the budget. Choose to be excited by what possibilities may be yours.

Maybe not a bearded dragon….. but you get the gist.

Reflect:

- Have I taken time to talk through budget needs with my leadership and understand their decisions?
- Am I willing to invest my finance into my ministry?
- Have I ever asked for miraculous provision?

Allyson Parker

Grasshoppers and Birthday Cake

It was my sister's birthday. She was turning 8 and my grandmother had come to visit. Mum had made a beautiful cake covered in pink fluffy frosting. The candles were lit and we were in the last strands of "Happy Birthday" when the grasshopper plague hit. Suddenly there was an incredible buzzing and grasshoppers undertook a kamikaze flight path through the flames and into the icing on top of the cake. Singed grasshopper has a distinctive smell. They do not add to cake.

There were grasshoppers everywhere, and my grandmother undertook a vigorous commitment to kill them with her slipper, which, while entertaining to watch, was a futile exercise and fairly short lived. Walking to the school bus now came with the unavoidable crunch of squashed grasshoppers underfoot (think multiplied cockroach squishing sound) and the boys on the bus discovered a whole new source of ammunition for the traditional 'pea shooter'- grasshopper heads. These were bitten off the bodies, added to an empty pen casing with some spit and aimed directly at your head. One learnt to dodge fairly quickly.

Driving in the car became almost impossible. Dad installed a wire mesh shield over the radiator and the windscreen. It was possible to drive for about 20 minutes before the screen became so embedded with grasshoppers that you could no longer see and you needed to pull over and bang the screen hard to dislodge the dead grasshoppers before proceeding again. Everything was eaten. Even washing on the clothes line. Then, as quickly as they came, they went.

Life and ministry can be a bit like this.

One minute you're celebrating. The next, out of nowhere, the enemy sweeps in unexpectedly and it seems as though everything is going to be destroyed. It could be a health issue, a grief or loss, a personal failure, or the heartache of a break down in team relationships. It can feel overwhelming.

I remember this moment for me. I was summoned to the home of a very key couple in the team- a couple I relied on considerably and whose leadership had brought the development of significant milestones in our ministry. They were creative, hard working and had close relationships with other key leaders. The meeting was not what I was expecting. I was met with a written list of my leadership and ministry failings and the reasons that they were leaving both the team and the church. Talk about the grasshopper plague landing. I felt sick to my stomach with anxiety, hurt, fear about what would happen to the team, and that awful sense of both rising pride and anger, alongside condemnation. Then there were the questions, 'Was everything they had said about me, true? Is that what everyone thinks?' It was one of the most difficult seasons of my life. But it was also a season where the 'rubber hit the road' in terms of applying some of the great principles Jesus taught us about responding to those who hurt us, mistreat us or are literally our enemies.

So what did I learn?

1. Keep going. Keep doing what you know to do. The grasshoppers came, but school went on, washing continued, dinner still had to be cooked. The same is true for us. Keep in the Word. Keep close to Jesus. Keep serving if you can.

2. Don't take what the enemy has put in your life and then shoot it at others around you through vindictive gossip. Stay sweet. Humble your heart. Ask for forgiveness. Be accountable for your failure with your leadership. Seek to grow. I prayed two scriptures into my life:

Psalm 139:23-24 New Living Translation (NLT)

23 Search me, O God, and know my heart; test me and know my anxious thoughts. 24 Point out anything in me that offends you, and lead me along the path of everlasting life.

Proverbs 26:2 New International Version (NIV)

2 Like a fluttering sparrow or a darting swallow, an undeserved curse does not come to rest.

Both prayers were equally important. I had to lay my heart and what I had been accused of before the throne room of heaven and humbly ask for Jesus' perspective. What I needed to repent of and what I needed to address in my attitudes and actions had to be dealt with.

I also needed to let go of that which was not true; that which was not me. I had to trust that God would protect me and the team from that which was undeserved.

3. I had to learn to halt the train of thought I had that was self-righteous and pride filled and make it back up to the station. I deliberately chose to pray blessing over them. In doing so, I discovered one of the great 'stealth bombs' against the enemy. Jesus doesn't ask us to 'bless those who curse us and pray for those who mistreat us' because he has some sort of malicious desire to torture us. It's because it begins to set us free- and the enemy doesn't expect it. When I first had to crunch on those grasshoppers on the way to the bus, it was hard and there was certainly a lot of squeamishness to my steps. But after a while, it became a challenge to see how many you could squish and destroy. I found that truly learning to delight in praying blessing brought joy, peace and hope for the future even though, initially, my flesh literally screamed, 'NO!'. (We crucify our flesh, people!)

4. Shield both your vision and your heart. The armour of God is not a cute Sunday lesson- it is the power of God for the battle. When it's hard to see, pull over- ask for help from those you trust. If you've shielded both your vision and your heart, you'll be able to clear them again. And again. And again. When your vision is based in 'why', you will find a way forward.

5. Remember that everything is temporary. It will pass.

None of us will ever be perfect leaders. We will fail. We will let people down. We will get it wrong. But we can all choose to be as much like Jesus as possible in the midst of it- and we will grow and mature if we let the trials so form us.

Those we lead, and those we minister to, need us to learn to overcome, persevere and keep standing, so we can teach them to do the same.

Reflect:

- How do I deal with criticism?
- How can I teach children to overcome and grow through challenges?

A Horse
Some Rain
Some Bread
and Home

It was a rare season of rain and the soil at Moree was black and impossible to drive on. In fact, it was impossible to walk on. I'm pretty certain the game 'stuck in the mud' was invented in an area of black soil. Due to the distance we lived from town, Mum only went grocery shopping once a month, and therefore the rain meant that, as we were nearing the end of the monthly supply of staples like bread and flour, we were unlikely to be able to replenish those supplies in the conventional way. We lived 11kms off the sealed highway that gave access to town, but the main homestead was only 1km off the highway and the road surface between the homestead and highway had been gravelled allowing some access. So Mum called the local supermarket and they agreed to find a way to deliver some much needed supplies to the homestead (initial click and collect). Once the groceries arrived, my sisters and I were dispatched on horseback to ride to the homestead and collect them in large calico flour bags tied to our backs. My bag was filled with sliced bread- sufficient to feed a family of 6 for a month.

22kms of riding is a good distance. It takes quite a number of hours. For 21 kms, all went well as the horses plodded along, but 1 km from home, my horse looked up, saw the house and decided that what was required was a sprint to the finish line.

He bolted. He took off at full pelt and headed directly for home- and nothing was going to stop him. I held on the reins and pulled as hard as I could, with no effect. Suddenly, my calico bag developed a split and slices of bread began to fan behind me like a tickertape parade. That was it. The precious cargo was at stake. That horse had to stop. There was a tree up ahead, so with a bit of quick judgement, and a sharp pull of the reins to the right, I turned him into the tree for a very abrupt halt (tree trunks will do that). Fortunately, we, and most of the bread, survived the experience. We made a controlled final 200m.

There are days in ministry where it just seems like you're getting nowhere or you are just plodding along.

The kids don't seem to respond and there's all sorts of behaviour issues and challenges.

Team are not turning up on time – or at all. There's no response to any form of communication and you despair that any parent will ever take note of what you do or what you plan.

It becomes discouraging and draining.

That's when you need to look up!

My favourite scripture says:

Colossians 3:1 New Living Translation (NLT)

> *3 Since you have been raised to new life with Christ, set your sights on the realities of heaven, where Christ sits in the place of honour at God's right hand*

When it gets discouraging, set your sight on heaven. Ask God for a new perspective to energise your soul.

The Message version says it like this:

Colossians 3:1-2 The Message (MSG)

> *1-2 So if you're serious about living this new resurrection life with Christ, act like it. Pursue the things over which Christ presides. Don't shuffle along, eyes to the ground, absorbed with the things right in front of you. Look up, and be alert to what is going on around Christ—that's where the action is. See things from his perspective.*

Maybe you've been doing children's ministry for 12 months or less- or maybe for 25 years or more. We all have days or seasons of discouragement. Go back to the cross. Spend time in worship. It's not the end of the story yet. Don't lose sight of 'home'. In my horse's brain and heart, HOME, suddenly broke through. The energy and focus that accompanied this was instant. It transformed his demeanour. It drove his decisions and the power of his movement.

There was a boy in our children's ministry who was challenging. He was full of energy and mischief and caused a number of strategic team meetings to plan how we would deal with his behaviour. When he was about 8 years old, in a time of the powerful Presence of the Holy Spirit, I prophesied over him that he would take on the mantle of children's ministry and become a Children's Pastor. The team in the room at the time looked at me as though some sort of madness had come over me! It seemed ludicrous. There was nothing to indicate that he would ever be involved in ministry. For years, that prophesy swirled in my head. Had I made a mistake? Had I spoken out something that was not from God? Did he even remember?

Last year, he, along with my youngest daughter who is now his wife, became our Kids' Service Pastors. Together, they lead our Sunday morning services across all age groups. It is just the start of what is ahead.

Look up. Fix your eyes on home. Let new energy surge into your present.

That kid, this season…… God's not finished yet.

Reflect:

- What helps me find new energy and strength when discouraged?
- How can I see what God sees in kids that are difficult?

Allyson Parker

Little Pink Pigs

I sat in my office dreaming about, and planning for new games for a big holiday program we had coming up, when a moment of inspiration hit me. All of a sudden I sat bolt upright and almost shouted, "I need little pink pigs! 100 of them." Then I slumped again as wondered where on earth I would find such a greatly needed resource, particularly within the budget I had to adhere to.

So I did what we all do and turned to Google. Right before my eyes came up an image of little pink pigs. Bags of 25 bath toy pink pigs about 3 cm long. They were perfect and available on Amazon AUSTRALIA well within my budget requirements. I almost heard the audible voice of Holy Spirit as He said, "Trust me." -because he knew in my heart I was saying, "I can't believe it."

Leadership can feel like pushing a loaded barrow uphill, or a constant battle. At times I've wondered if there is any 'resting point', or if it gets any easier.

Truthfully, great leaders should always be 'pushing uphill'- leading others to new places, carrying the load of vision and purpose. If it is all easy going, then probably nothing new has been birthed for a while, and potentially there's no new steps of faith and growth being pursued. (However, let me encourage you, that experience does help along the way!) So don't ease away from the 'push'- let it strengthen you.

If there's a battle, remember ALWAYS:

Ephesians 6:12 Easy-to-Read Version (ERV)

> *12 Our fight is not against people on earth. We are fighting against the rulers and authorities and the powers of this world's darkness. We are fighting against the spiritual powers of evil in the heavenly places*

Take your battle to your knees before you take it anywhere else.

Why would the King of Heaven care about little pink pigs?

Because he delights in us. He delights in our kids. And he delights in providing what we need.

My box of little pink pigs arrived and it was one of the most fun packages I've ever opened. There was something ridiculously exciting about getting it. I think it simply had the smile of heaven imprinted on it.

My little pigs have now become the perfect object lesson for the Parable of the Lost Sheep because there's only 99 in their storage container. No, one is not lost. I have one perpetually in my office to remind me on the days when the question rises, "how am I going to do this?", that I'm not doing this alone.

And that the smile of Heaven is over me.

In the load of leadership, the smile of heaven is still over you! You are the focus of the Father. Don't let the load cause you to lose the truth. Don't let the burden allow the enemy to add a brick of "you don't matter" to all you carry.

Romans 8:15 The Passion Translation (TPT)

^{15} And you did not receive the "spirit of religious duty," leading you back into the fear of never being good enough. But you have received the "Spirit of full acceptance," enfolding you into the family of God. And you will never feel orphaned, for as he rises up within us, our spirits join him in saying the words of tender affection, "Beloved Father!"

Dad loves you. He is for you. The smile of heaven IS over you.

We can sometimes forget this, especially if we feel that we are unnoticed by our church, or that we have no voice within our organization or that our team won't commit, or what is asked of us is too much, or life is just overwhelming. These emotions happen to the best of us. Emotions are terrible faith bearers!

You're not alone. You're not unnoticed. You matter in the Kingdom. What you do- laying faith foundations in the next generation- it's far too important for you to quit. Your Father in heaven is not going to give you a stone if you ask for a fish!

From team to toys, to budgets, to time, to little pink pigs- He's got you! And he won't let you go.

Reflect:

- Do I believe that God is for me?
- Do I believe that the smile of heaven is over my ministry?
- What would change if I did believe that God was as interested and committed to all I was doing in children's ministry as he was in the ministry of the Senior Pastor?

Allyson Parker

Sleepwalking dilemmas

We had a kids' overnight event. One of our teenage leaders was sleeping at the entrance of the rooms with the girls. In the middle of the night she awoke suddenly as a child tapped her on the shoulder and said, "Excuse me, I need some help." Before she had any time to properly respond, the child promptly proceeded to pee on her before returning to bed.

Have you ever tried to get out of a sleeping bag at speed?

Yeah… Nah… Not possible.

"She was not the one who needed help!" This sentence continues to make me laugh with inappropriate delight.

Nothing else.

It's just a great story.

Go bless the House of God.

Allyson Parker

For more information contact:

Advantage Books
P.O. Box 160847
Altamonte Springs, FL 32716
info@advbooks.com

To purchase additional copies of these books, visit our bookstore at:
www.advbookstore.com

Longwood, Florida, USA
"we bring dreams to life"™
www.advbookstore.com

www.ingramcontent.com/pod-product-compliance
Lightning Source LLC
Chambersburg PA
CBHW061255040426
42444CB00010B/2388